To

*a gift to help you open
your heart to the beauty
and mystery of life.*

From

THE BEDSIDE BOOK OF

ANGELS

CONTRIBUTING WRITER
Anna Trimiew

PUBLICATIONS INTERNATIONAL, LTD.

Louis Weber, C.E.O.
Publications International, Ltd.
7373 North Cicero Avenue
Lincolnwood, Illinois 60646

Manufactured in China.

8 7 6 5 4 3 2 1

ISBN: 0-7853-2162-4

Many of the selections in this book were written by Anna Trimiew, a freelance writer and former schoolteacher who holds a master's degree from Gordon-Cronwell Theological Seminary. Her previously published work includes *Who's Who in the Bible*, *The Bible Almanac*, *Pocket Inspirations*, and *Bringing the New Testament to Life*.

Contents

Angels
Among Us

Angels surround our
lives with love and protection.
Know that they are among us
to ease our burdens, shield us
from evil, lighten our hearts,
and guide us along our
journey.

We pray for heavenly protection; we put ourselves into [God's] hands when we go on a journey; we commit our loved ones into His care and keeping. But how little we know how graciously our prayers and our trust in Him are answered in a supernatural manner by ministering angels.

ARNO CLEMENS GAEBELIN,
THE ANGELS OF GOD

◆

ANGELS AMONG US

ANGELS AMONG US

*Sweet souls around
us watch us still,
Press nearer to our side;
Into our thoughts, into
our prayers,
With gentle helpings
glide.*

HARRIET BEECHER STOWE, FROM
"THE OTHER WORLD"

◆

ANGELS AMONG US

OVER MY HEAD

Over my head—
I hear music in the air…
Over my head—I hear
singing in the air…
There must be a God
somewhere.

TRADITIONAL SPIRITUAL

◆

ANGELS AMONG US

ANGELS AMONG US

*I*f you pray truly,
you will feel within
yourself a great
assurance, and the angels
will be your companions.

EVAGRIUS OF PONTUS, FROM
SEASONS OF THE SPIRIT

◆

ANGELS AMONG US

Lord, send your
swift angels to smooth
out our wrinkled brows.
Encircle our night with
the wings of your
protection, so that we
may rest quietly, content
in your watchful care.

◆

ANGEL PRESENCE

Wing and harp
and robe of white,
Sliding through the day
and night,
Spirit beings bathed
in light,
Invisible among us.
We walk by faith,
not sight.

ANGELS AMONG US

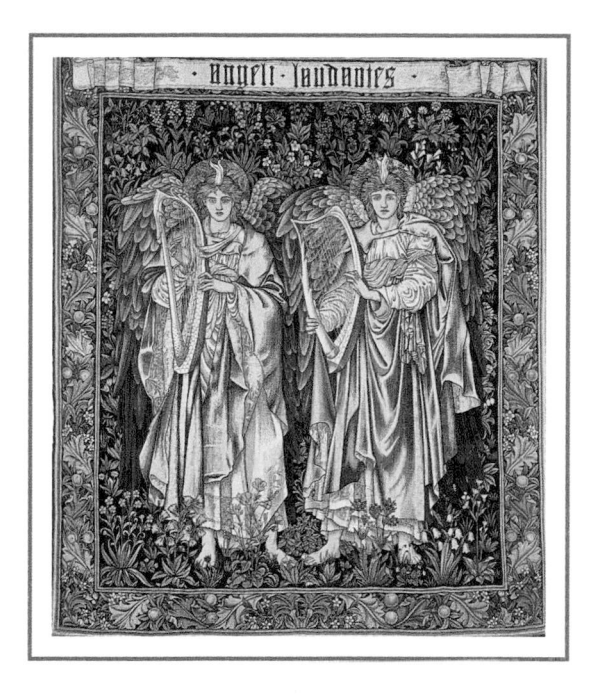

ANGELS AMONG US

Angels are the
ministers and the dispensers of
the divine bounty toward us.
Accordingly, we are told how
they watch for our safety, how
they undertake our defence,
direct our path, and take heed
that no evil befall us.

JOHN CALVIN, *INSTITUTES OF THE
CHRISTIAN RELIGION*, Vol. I

◆

ANGELS AMONG US

ANGELS AMONG US

Paula had been sleeping restlessly for several hours, when suddenly she awakened. There, again, was the light that had come to her several months ago. "It was brighter than the sun, coming from the ceiling, saturating the dark room from the top down," Paula says. But instead of sorrow, she felt an

◆

ANGELS AMONG US

indescribable jubilance. The light filled her, wrapping her with warmth and reassurance, soothing her broken heart as she watched it, welcomed it, basked in it. "I got a message, though not in words, that I should go on, and everything would be all right."

JOAN WESTER ANDERSON,
WHERE MIRACLES HAPPEN

◆

ANGELS AMONG US

An angel can illumine the thought and mind of man by strengthening the power of vision, and by bringing within its reach some truth which the angel himself contemplates.

ST. THOMAS AQUINAS

◆

ANGELS AMONG US

ANGELS AMONG US

CELESTIAL
MESSENGERS

Angels carry messages
from heaven to earth. God
uses his angels to tell us of his
mercy and to show us the way
he wants us to go.

Celestial beings, messengers of light, the neighbor next door, even a passing stranger— angels appear in many forms. Be open to receive them, for they come to us on heavenly business.

◆

CELESTIAL MESSENGERS

*L*auren's grandpa was ill, and he died in the hospital. Lauren's mom, an emergency technician, tried to comfort her four-year-old daughter in the weeks following his death, but she realized that Lauren continued to be troubled. The little girl was afraid that mom would die at the hospital, just like grandpa did. One night Lauren had a wonderful dream that grandpa and an angel came

◆

to her bedside. Grandpa smiled at Lauren and told her that he was fine, and that he was living with Jesus and the angels. After grandpa and the angel left the room, Lauren's young heart lifted. She felt secure now, knowing that grandpa was okay, and that mom would be safe working at the hospital.

ELLEN CURTIS, STORE MANAGER

◆

CELESTIAL MESSENGERS

CELESTIAL MESSENGERS

*L*ord, you come to us in the storm,
the fire, and even in the stillness of a
quiet moment. Sometimes your message
is strong, carried on bustling angelic
wings; sometimes our spirits are nudged,
our hearts lightened by the gentle
whisper of spirit voices. However you
approach us, your message is always one
of tender love and compassion.
Thank you for the certainty—and the
surprise—of your holy voice.

CELESTIAL MESSENGERS

While Abraham was grazing his flocks on the plain of Mamre, three angels arrived to remind him of God's promise that he and his wife would be blessed with a child: They did not appear in their own bright form, but as three travelers. They came in the heat of the day...they were dusty and stained with travel. But Abraham immediately recognized them as coming from the Lord.

BERNARD EVSLIN,
SIGNS AND WONDERS

CELESTIAL MESSENGERS

*A*s I walked along the beach, I asked God for a special revelation of himself. I longed for a unique sense of his closeness, a personal touch. Suddenly the words were before me—*I love you, Joy*—neatly carved into the smooth, wet sand, each letter perfectly formed. I knew the words had come from God himself, put there by one of his ministering angels, just for me. My heart and faith were uplifted by this simple miracle, one which I often recall and will forever treasure.

JOY BANTA, SECRETARY

*I*t warms my heart to know that my family is safe in the capable hands of angels. They are their watchful companions, whispering encouragements and words of warning, protecting them from harm.

I imagine these busy guardians going about their work, and I feel blessed.

HEATHER GRAHAM POZZESSERE,
AN ANGEL'S TOUCH

CELESTIAL MESSENGERS

CELESTIAL MESSENGERS

GLORIOUS
BEINGS

Who are these godly
beings that minister to us?
They are wise and wonderful
personalities that come before
us in visions, in dreams,
and in person.

◆

*A*ngels speak. They appear and reappear. They feel with apt sense of emotion. While angels might become visible by choice, our eyes are not constructed to see them ordinarily. . . .

BILLY GRAHAM,
ANGELS: GOD'S SECRET AGENTS

GLORIOUS BEINGS

ANGELS

Bright beings,
dazzling as lightning
Glorious angels,
shimmering like the sun
Powerful spirits,
descending from heaven
Swift presence,
visible and invisible.

◆

GLORIOUS BEINGS

GLORIOUS BEINGS

I swerved helplessly on the icy,
desolate road. Caught in a hopeless skid,
the car finally came to a stop in a ditch.
Although unharmed, I knew I was stuck
miles from home on this frigid winter
night. Surprisingly, moments later, a car
appeared from nowhere, and the driver
offered to help.

As we rode to safety, I had a burning
sense of spiritual kinship with my good

◆

GLORIOUS BEINGS

samaritan. We exchanged addresses, and I promised to be in touch. Later, when I tried, my card to him was returned undelivered. And when I inquired, no one in this small Indiana community seemed to know him. Was he an angel in disguise who had disappeared as simply and quietly as he had appeared?

PAULA GAST, THERAPIST

◆

GLORIOUS BEINGS

GLORIOUS BEINGS

Daniel's vision of the last days begins with the awesome appearance of a celestial being, probably Gabriel:

I looked up, and there before me was a man dressed in linen, with a belt of the finest gold around his waist. His body was like chrysolite, his face like lightning, his eyes like flaming torches, his arms and legs like the gleam of burnished bronze, and his voice like the sound of a multitude.

I, Daniel, was the only one who saw the vision; the men with me did not see it,

GLORIOUS BEINGS

but such terror overwhelmed them that
they fled and hid themselves. So I was
left alone, gazing at this great vision; I
had no strength left, my face turned
deathly pale and I was helpless. Then I
heard him speaking, and as I listened to
him, I fell into a deep sleep, my face to
the ground.

DANIEL 10:5–9,
NEW INTERNATIONAL VERSION

◆

GLORIOUS BEINGS

I have seen
a thousand times
that angels are
human forms... for
I have conversed with
them... sometimes with
one alone, sometimes
with many in company.

EMANUEL SWEDENBORG
(1688–1772), SWEDISH
THEOLOGIAN

GLORIOUS BEINGS

GLORIOUS BEINGS

MICHAEL AND GABRIEL

Michael, the first
angel—prince and principal,
in tandem with God's heroic
messenger of mercy
and promise, dependable
Gabriel; swiftly they move,
crafting visions and dreams,
words and actions. . . .
We reel in their wake,
transformed by the divine.

◆

GLORIOUS BEINGS

The night before Herod was to bring
him to trial, Peter was sleeping between
two soldiers, bound with two chains, and
sentries stood guard at the entrance.
Suddenly an angel of the Lord appeared,
and a light shone in the cell. He struck
Peter on the side and woke him up.
"Quick, get up!" he said, and the chains
fell off Peter's wrists.

ACTS 12:6–7,
NEW INTERNATIONAL VERSION

◆

GLORIOUS BEINGS

GLORIOUS BEINGS

ANGELIC ENCOUNTERS

*I*n a moment of quiet, dark stillness, or even in the bustle of daily life, you may occasionally feel that you are in the company of an angel. Revel in its divine presence!

An angel stood and
met my gaze,
Through the low doorway
of my tent;
The tent is struck,
the vision stays;
I only know she came
and went.

J. R. LOWELL (1819–1891),
AMERICAN POET, FROM
"SHE CAME AND WENT"

ANGELIC ENCOUNTERS

*A*ngels move in mysterious and wonderful ways. They speak with hushed and holy voices, and in warm and gentle tones. Their loving presence and kind words cover us with peace and comfort.

◆

ANGELIC ENCOUNTERS

ANGELIC ENCOUNTERS

The guardian
angels of life sometimes
fly so high as to be
beyond our sight, but they
are always looking down
upon us.

JEAN PAUL RICHTER
(1763–1825), GERMAN WRITER

◆

*H*ave you ever felt your spirit
quicken, a sense that you are being
directed a certain way?...
I was particularly tired when I came
home from work late one night. I crawled
into bed with a prayer that my guardian
angel would protect my dear, disabled
husband already asleep in his own
bedroom, specially set up for his medical
and physical needs. It was about
midnight, and sleep came easily.
Next morning, my husband told me that
late the night before he had felt the side

of the bed give, and he groped around,
thinking it was a visit from the family
dog. But it wasn't. Then he heard
someone say, "Are you okay?" He
answered "yes" and fell asleep.
"Did you come in to check on me at
midnight?" he wanted to know. I smiled
knowingly, grateful that my guardian
angel had honored my request, and
gently seen to my husband's needs.

ELLEN CURTIS, STORE MANAGER

ANGELIC ENCOUNTERS

*E*ven while I was praying and confessing my sin and the sins of my people, and desperately pleading with the Lord my God for Jerusalem, his holy mountain, Gabriel, whom I had seen in the earlier vision, flew swiftly to me at the time of the evening sacrifice, and said to me, "Daniel, I am here to help you understand God's plans . . . God loves you very much."

DANIEL 9:20–23,
THE LIVING BIBLE

ANGELIC ENCOUNTERS

ANGELIC ENCOUNTERS

55

To sense the
presence of an angel
is like feeling the wind
all around you.
You cannot actually see
the wind, but you notice
its movement, and you
know that it is there.

◆

*I*f you have the good fortune to be surprised by an angel, you will enjoy a delightful, lingering sense of the divine. Indeed, your life will never be ordinary again.

◆

GAZING AT HEAVEN

$\mathcal{A}$ngels reflect the magnificence of heaven, the spectacular home that God has prepared for all those who belong to him.

◆

BLESSED ASSURANCE

*P*erfect submission,
perfect delight!
Visions of rapture now
burst on my sight;
Angels descending
bring from above,
Echoes of mercy,
whispers of love.

FANNY J. CROSBY, *THE HYMNAL*

◆

GAZING AT HEAVEN

I want to be
an angel,
And with the angels
stand,
A crown upon my
forehead,
A harp within my hand.

URANIA BAILEY,
I WANT TO BE AN ANGEL (1850)

◆

GAZING AT HEAVEN

Gazing at Heaven

A friend of mine told me about her mother's death from cancer. "My mother died two years ago. She actually came to the Lord during the time of her illness. The night she died, my sister was near her bed. She was astonished to see my mother surrounded by a brilliant light. She said it looked like the aurora borealis. She was sure it was the angels."

ANN SPANGLER,
AN ANGEL A DAY

◆

GAZING AT HEAVEN

GAZING AT HEAVEN

GAZING AT HEAVEN

But all God's angels
come to us disguised;
Sorrow and sickness,
poverty and death,
One after other lift their
frowning masks,
And we behold the Seraph's
face beneath,
All radiant with the glory and
the calm
Of having looked upon the
front of God.

J. R. LOWELL, FROM "ON THE
DEATH OF A FRIEND'S CHILD"

GAZING AT HEAVEN

GAZING AT HEAVEN

Heaven abounds
with angels of light.
When our life on earth is
over, they will whisk us
there to experience for
ourselves the glorious
perfection of eternal life.

◆

*I*n heaven, the
angelic choir sings, and a
bright hosanna of music
flows and swells
throughout the Holy
City. It is the perfect and
glorious beginning to an
endless day.

◆

ACKNOWLEDGEMENTS

Pages 16-17: From the book *Where Miracles Happen: True Stories of Heavenly Encounters* by Joan Wester Anderson. Copyright © 1994 by Joan Wester Anderson. Published by Brett Books, Inc. Reprinted by permission.

PHOTO CREDITS

The Crosiers: 15, 31, 35, 42, 55, 63, 66, 73; **Superstock:** 6, 27, 38, 68, 70; Christie's London: 9, 56, 65; David David Gallery: 24, 50; The Huntington, San Marino, California: 45; Pinacoteca Di Brera, Milan, Italy: 59; Pinacoteca Tosio Martinengo, Brescia, 19; **Victoria & Albert Museum/Art Resource:** 13.

Cover photo: "The Guardian Angel," Wilhelm Von Kaulbach/**Superstock.**

73